OUR PURPOSE IS LOVE:
THE WESLEYAN WAY TO BE THE CHURCH
LEADER GUIDE

LEADER GUIDE

our purpose is

love

the Wesleyan way to be the church

David N. Field

Leader Guide by Barbara Dick

Abingdon Press / Nashville

Our Purpose Is Love:
The Wesleyan Way to Be the Church
Leader Guide

ISBN 978-1-5018-6869-6

Scripture quotations are taken from the Common English Bible, copyright 2011. Used by permission. All rights reserved.

18 19 20 21 22 23 24 25 26 27—10 9 8 7 6 5 4 3 2 1
MANUFACTURED in the UNITED STATES of AMERICA

CONTENTS

TO THE LEADER

Welcome! In this study you have the opportunity to help a group explore love as the driving purpose of human life, with insights and wisdom from the Bible and from the founder of Methodism, John Wesley. David N. Field, the author of *Our Purpose Is Love*, helps us move from a general understanding of the nature of love to the specific ways the church is called to embody and offer love in and to the world.

These are fundamental, large concepts, that will require considerable focus and attention. Significant questions of personal accountability and, perhaps, failure may arise in the course of your sessions. There may also be disagreement as group members address topics that can be divisive at times. Consider how to create the kind of safe learning environment in which participants can share their experiences and feelings honestly, as well as listen to others with sensitivity.

Scripture tells us that where two or three are gathered together, we can be assured of the presence of the Holy Spirit, working in and through all those gathered. As you prepare to lead, pray for that presence and expect that you will experience it.

This eight- or nine-session study (see below) makes use of the following components:

- the study book, *Our Purpose Is Love: The Wesleyan Way to Be the Church* by David N. Field
- this *Leader Guide*
- John Wesley's writings. Recommended resources include:
  ◊ Print: *The Bicentennial Edition of the Works of John Wesley* [hereafter *Works*], gen. ed. Albert C. Outler, published by Abingdon Press. Material continues to be added to this multivolume collection. Your church library may have some volumes available for use by the group.
  ◊ Online: Northwest Nazarene University offers a comprehensive collection of Wesley's sermons, letters, and notes. The collection draws on the "Jackson" edition of *The Works of John Wesley* [hereafter *Works* (Jackson)]; http://wesley.nnu.edu/john-wesley.

Participants in the study will also need Bibles, as well as either a spiral-bound journal or an electronic means of journaling, such as a tablet. Make arrangements for participants to get copies of the book in advance, so that they can read chapter 1 before the first session.

Using This Guide with Your Group

Because no two groups are alike, this guide has been designed to give you flexibility and choice in tailoring the sessions for your group. The session format is listed below. You may choose any or all of the activities, adapting them as you wish to meet the schedule and needs of your particular group.

You may choose to complete this study in eight or nine sessions as your group schedule permits. The ninth session is an optional opportunity to review the learnings from the earlier sessions and to share in a closing ritual with the group. Notes in sessions 8 and 9 will help guide you in whichever option you choose.

Most session time will be too short to do all the activities. Select ahead of time which activities the group will do, for how long, and in what order. In some sessions, video clips or music selections are suggested. While these resources can give participants a multi-sensory experience, they are not essential to the study. Depending on which activities you select, there may be special preparation needed. The leader is alerted to what is needed up front in the session plan.

Session Format

Planning the Session

Session Goals
Biblical Foundation
Special Preparation

Getting Started

Opening Activity
Opening Prayer

Learning Together

Bible Study and Discussion
Book Study and Discussion

Wrapping Up

Closing Activity
Closing Prayer

Helpful Hints

Preparing for the Session

- Pray for the leading of the Holy Spirit as you prepare for the study. Pray for discernment for yourself and for each member of the study group.
- Before each session, familiarize yourself with the content. Read the book chapter again.
- Choose the session elements you will use during the group session, including the specific discussion questions you plan to cover. Be prepared, however, to adjust the session as group members interact and as questions arise. Prepare carefully, but allow space for the Holy Spirit to move in and through the group members and through you as facilitator.
- If you plan to use video clips or music suggestions, obtain appropriate projection equipment and test it before the session in which you plan to use it.
- Prepare the space where the group will meet so that the space will enhance the learning process. Ideally, group members should be seated around a table or in a circle so that all can see one another. Movable chairs are best, because the group will often form pairs or small groups for discussion.
- Bring a supply of Bibles for those who forget to bring their own. Provide a variety of translations.

- For most sessions, you will also need an easel with paper and markers, a whiteboard and markers, or some other means of posting group questions and responses.

Shaping the Learning Environment

- Begin and end on time.
- Establish a welcoming space. Consider the room temperature, access to amenities, hospitality, outside noise, and privacy. Use a small cross or candle as a focal point for times of prayer.
- Create a climate of openness, encouraging group members to participate as they feel comfortable. Be on the lookout for signs of discomfort in those who may be silent, and encourage them to express their thoughts and feelings honestly. But assure the group members that passing on a question is always acceptable.
- Remember that some people will jump right in with answers and comments, while others need time to process what is being discussed.
- If you notice that some group members seem never to be able to enter the conversation, ask them if they have thoughts to share. Give everyone a chance to talk, but keep the conversation moving. Moderate to prevent a few individuals from doing all the talking.
- Make use of the exercises that invite sharing in pairs. Those who are reluctant to speak out in a group setting may be more comfortable sharing one-on-one and reporting back to the group. This can often be an effective means of helping people grow more comfortable sharing in the larger setting. It also helps avoid the dominance of the group by one or two participants (including you!).

- If no one answers at first during discussions, do not be afraid of silence. Help the group become comfortable with waiting. If no one responds, try reframing the language of the question. If no responses are forthcoming, venture an answer yourself and ask for comments.
- Model openness as you share with the group. Group members will follow your example. If you limit your sharing to a surface level, others will follow suit.
- Encourage multiple answers or responses before moving on.
- Ask, "Why?" or "Why do you believe that?" or "Can you say more about that?" to help continue a discussion and give it greater depth.
- Affirm others' responses with comments such as "Great" or "Thanks" or "Good insight"—especially if it's the first time someone has spoken during the group session.
- Monitor your own contributions. If you are doing most of the talking, back off so that you do not train the group to listen rather than speak up.
- Remember that you do not have all the answers. Your job is to keep the discussion going and encourage participation.

Managing the Session

- Honor the time schedule. If a session is running longer than expected, get consensus from the group before continuing beyond the agreed-upon ending time.
- When someone arrives late or *must* leave early, pause the session *briefly* to welcome them or bid them farewell. Changes in the makeup of the group change the dynamics

of the discussion and need to be acknowledged. Every group member is important to the entire group.

- Involve group members in various aspects of the group session, such as saying prayers or reading the Scripture.
- As always in discussions that may involve personal sharing, confidentiality is essential. Group members should never pass along stories that have been shared in the group. Remind the group members at each session: confidentiality is crucial to the success of this study.

One
WHY IS LOVE THE ANSWER?

Planning the Session

Session Goals

As a result of conversations and activities connected with this session, group members should begin to:

- Reflect on biblical passages related to the character of God, the nature of love, and God's purpose for humanity.
- Understand the meaning of *love* and *purpose.*
- Assess their relationship with God and neighbor.
- Explore John Wesley's teachings on the nature of love and purpose.

Biblical Foundation

> God created humanity in God's own image,
>> in the divine image God created them,
>>> male and female God created them. (Gen 1:27)

Special Preparation

- If possible in advance of the first session, ask participants to bring either a spiral-bound notebook or an electronic means of journaling, such as a tablet. Provide writing paper and pens for those who may need them. Also have a variety of Bibles available for those who do not bring one.
- Make sure all participants have a copy of the study book, *Our Purpose Is Love*. Invite them to read chapter 1 in advance of the first session. You also should read this material.
- On a large sheet of paper or a board, print the following at the top: "*Love* is . . ."
- On another sheet, print: "*Purpose* means . . ."
- Have available large sheets of blank paper (newsprint) or construction paper and colored markers for group activity.
- Depending on the size of your space, post some or all of the following Scripture references: Gen 1:27; Ps 86:15; Jer 31:33-34; Matt 5:43-48; 1 John 4:8.

Remember that there are more activities than most groups will have time to complete. As leader, you'll want to go over the session in advance and select or adapt the activities you think will work best for your group in the time allotted. Consider your own responses to questions you will pose to the group.

If group members are not familiar with one another, make nametags available.

Getting Started

Welcome

As participants arrive, welcome them to the study and invite them to make use of one of the available Bibles, if they did not bring one.

Opening Prayer

Gracious and loving God, as we begin this study, open us to your presence and fill us—our time, our conversations, our reflections, our doubts, and our fears—with the joy of exploration and the wisdom of your love. We gather together in Jesus' name. Amen.

Opening Activity

When all participants have arrived, invite each person to introduce himself or herself by name and to complete one of the posted prompts ("*Love* is . . ." or "*Purpose* means . . ."). Do not take notes during the introductions. When the circle is complete, invite general responses to each of the prompts and post them on the sheet (or whiteboard). Participants may repeat their original response or add to it. Defining these terms provides a foundation and starting place for the study. Invite participants to add comments and new understandings to these definitions and lists during the weeks of the study.

Learning Together

Bible Study and Discussion

Throughout chapter 1, the author explores the nature of God, love, and God's purpose for humanity. Invite participants to form pairs. Each pair will take five minutes to read one of the following passages and share what it teaches. It is unlikely that you will assign all of the passages; assign at least the readings from Gen 1 and 1 John 4:8, and expand from there as your group size permits:

- Gen 1:27
- Exod 23:10-11
- Ps 86:15
- Jer 31:33-34
- Matt 5:43-48
- Col 1:15
- 1 John 4:8

Invite the pairs back to the larger group to share insights from their conversations. If the group wants to add any of the new ideas or insights to the posted group "definition" of *love*, invite participants to do so.

Created in God's Image

Invite participants to reflect on the following questions and then share their responses with the group or note them in their journals.

- If you were to describe the character of God in a short sentence, what would you write?
- What does it mean to be created in God's image?
- What insights from John Wesley does the author offer in answering these questions?

Book Study and Discussion

God's Love

In the section entitled "Who Is God? and What Is God Like?" the author offers some biblical and Wesleyan insights on the nature of

God's love. Invite a group member to read the section that begins: "From the Bible and Wesleyan theology, we see that...," including the list of four perspectives (pages 15–16). Form four small groups of participants, and assign one of the perspectives to each. Invite each group to make a list of examples where they see or experience that aspect of God's love. Note that some of the examples may be stated in the negative (for example, God's love is absent in times of injustice; people who act from self-interest deny the power of God's love on the cross). Invite participants to be specific in their examples.

- God's love is relational.
- God's love is expressed in mercy, justice, and truth.
- God's love is most profoundly revealed on the cross.
- God's love is not opposed to God's anger, because God's anger protects.

Give the small groups some time to work, and then invite them to share their lists with the larger group.

Human Love

In the section "Loving God and Others," the author states, "Love should motivate and shape all of our attitudes, thoughts, words, and actions. Yet in our culture today, love has been devalued.... [L]ove is reduced to being nice, not rocking the boat, and pretending that problems do not exist" (page 17). Invite a volunteer to read that first paragraph aloud. Ask participants in what ways they agree or disagree with the author's assessment of *love* as it is expressed in today's culture.

Wesley on Grace

A theme that will recur throughout the study is Wesley's focus on God's grace. It is a defining characteristic of Methodism. Chapter 1 introduces the Wesleyan concept of *prevenient grace* and explores the general nature of *grace*. Invite a volunteer to read the summary list of aspects of grace under the heading "God's Mission in the World" (pages 20–21). Ask participants to share, in pairs, their responses to the list.

Wesley and Law

Another recurring theme is introduced in chapter 1: Wesley's concepts of *justice, mercy*, and *truth*, as requirements of the *moral law*. Take turns reading aloud through the section "God, Israel, and Love in the Bible" on page 22. (Remember, it is always permissible for a group member to say no to an invitation to read aloud.) Ask participants to share what terms or ideas spark their interest. Encourage participants to read, on their own, the Old Testament texts related to the example of the law, lifted up by the author, of the Sabbatical and Jubilee years.

Wesley and the New Creation

The final concept explored in this first chapter is the dramatic transformation of humanity made possible in the life, death, and resurrection of Jesus the Christ. The author offers a variety of perspectives on the "new thing" God does in Christ. As humanity fails again and again, God does not give up, but gives us new ways to fulfill the promise of love. Invite a volunteer to read the excerpt from Wesley's sermon, "Scriptural Christianity." The author states that "[t]his vision was no more realistic in Wesley's time than it is today" (page 29). Invite group members to share, in pairs, ways that United Methodists and others in their context are actively embodying God's love for the world. In what ways are they denying that love?

Wrapping Up

Closing Activities

Personal Reflection

In the section "Loving God and Others" (page 17), the author offers a list of key features of biblical love. Invite participants to take some time to read through and reflect on the list and note in their journals where they see themselves. In what aspect of love are they thriving? Where is there room for improvement?

- Love for God is centering one's life on God—giving God ultimate loyalty, living one's life to God's glory, and rejecting all competing loyalties.
- Love for God is not of obligation; it arises out of gratitude for all that God has done in Christ, and it involves the whole of our being.
- Love for God is embodied in a life of prayer and thanksgiving, participation in communal worship, obedience to God's commandments, and trust in God's care.
- Love for others is the self-sacrificial commitment to the concrete and holistic well-being of all human beings, which includes spiritual, psychological, physical, and social dimensions.
- Love for others is not mere outward actions; it involves inner attitudes and motivations such as patience, humility, meekness, justice, self-sacrifice, and benevolence.
- Love for God gives rise to a concern for the earth and a care for its creatures, for these were created by God and are the subject of God's concern and care.

Give some quiet time for this activity, and then invite group members to share one or two insights from their reflections. Remember, all responses are valid, and not sharing is always an option.

Preparation for Session Two

Read together the opening paragraph of chapter 2 and encourage participants to consider their responses as they read chapter 2. Remind them to note new insights and questions that develop as they read.

Closing Prayer

God of creation and never-failing love, fill us with your power as we leave this place, so that all we have shared and learned here helps us to be more faithful stewards of your grace. As your church in and for the world, we pray in the name of Jesus the Christ. Amen.

Two

A LIFE SATURATED WITH THE LOVE OF GOD

Planning the Session

Session Goals

As a result of conversations and activities connected with this session, group members should begin to:

- Reflect on biblical passages related to loving God and neighbor.
- Understand what it means to be "permeated by love."
- Assess the extent to which their lives are saturated with the love of God.
- Explore John Wesley's teachings on justification, sanctification, and perfection.

Biblical Foundation

> *"You must love the Lord your God with all your heart,*
> *with all your being, with all your strength, and with all*
> *your mind, and love your neighbor as yourself."*
>
> (Luke 10:27)

Special Preparation

- Ask participants to bring their notebooks or electronic journals. Provide writing paper and pens for those who may need them. Also have a variety of Bibles available for those who do not bring one.
- Invite participants to consider one insight they might want to share with the group from their closing meditation in session 1.
- Have available blank paper or construction paper and markers or crayons.
- Have a large sheet of paper or whiteboard available for group activity.

Remember that there are more activities than most groups will have time to complete. As leader, you'll want to go over the session in advance and select or adapt the activities you think will work best for your group in the time allotted. Consider your own responses to questions you will pose to the group.

If group members are not familiar with one another, make nametags available.

Getting Started

Welcome

As participants arrive, welcome them to the study and invite them to make use of one of the available Bibles, if they did not bring one.

Opening Prayer

Calling God, we gather here to know you better, to learn ways for our lives to be more attuned to your will. Open us to your presence and assurance as we share our doubts and failings, our experiences and knowledge. We humbly rely on you, Lord, and we pray in Jesus' name. Amen.

Opening Activities

What Is a Christian?

When all participants have arrived, invite each person to introduce himself or herself by name and to share his or her one-sentence response to the "elevator" question at the start of this chapter: "What is a Christian?" Do not take notes during the introductions. When the circle is complete, ask participants if they were surprised by any of the responses. How did the responses differ? What did they have in common? Compare the responses with the author's use of Wesley's expression, "a Christian is one who has the 'mind of Christ' (that is, a mind permeated by love) and walks as Jesus did."

How Is It with Your Soul?

Invite participants to spend a few moments in silent reflection on their relationship with God. Ask them to remember times and occasions when they have been particularly aware of God's presence in their lives. What are the particular things that they are grateful to God for? Maybe they are not feeling very close to God at present. Someone might even be angry with God. Assure them that this happens to us all. Remind them that there numerous passages in the Bible, particularly in Psalms, where the authors express frustration, complaint, and even anger to God. Having reflected on their relationship with God, invite each person to spend a few minutes in prayer, bringing this all to God.

Learning Together

Bible Study and Discussion

A Life Shaped by Love

In the section "Attitudes, Words, and Actions" (page 39), the author lists some of the attributes Wesley used to describe a life shaped by love. Form four small teams, and assign each team one of the following Bible passages:

- Rom 12:9-21
- 1 Cor 13:4-13
- Gal 5:22-24
- Phil 4:4-9

Ask each team to compare Wesley's list with the attributes in their assigned Bible passage. What do they have in common? What is unique to each? Ask the teams to prioritize the attributes from most important to least important (expect them to struggle with this and, perhaps, push back about relative importance in different contexts). Distribute large sheets of paper or construction paper and markers, and ask each team to choose a spokesperson.

Invite the teams back together to share their lists and the collective wisdom from their conversations.

Love God and Neighbor

In chapter 1, we explored the nature of love. Chapter 2 explores the requirements for living a life shaped by love. Invite a volunteer to read aloud Luke 10:27. Share with the group that Jesus was quoting the Old Testament in these two commandments: Deut 6:5 and Lev 19:18. Invite volunteers to read these verses aloud. Now invite another volunteer to read aloud the Ten Commandments from Exod 20:1-17.

Invite participants, in pairs, to consider the relationship between the two commandments of Jesus and the Ten Commandments. When the pairs have had some time to share, invite responses and insights.

With these insights in mind, invite a volunteer to read this statement from the section "A Life Shaped by Love" (pages 34–36):

> It is never enough to do good as a means to be well thought
> of and to gain favor. Kind and helpful acts may never create
> in us a heart full of love, but a heart filled with love will
> always move a Christian to kind and helpful action.

Ask participants in what ways they agree or disagree with the statement.

Book Study and Discussion

Truth, Justice, and Mercy

In the section "Attitudes, Words, and Actions" (page 39), the author explores the social-justice dimensions of a life permeated by love, revisiting the Wesleyan concepts of *truth, justice,* and *mercy.* Invite volunteers to read aloud the section that begins "*Truth* is the first criterion of loving words" (pages 40–41). Post the following questions and ask participants to consider them as they hear the section read. Suggest that they make notes in their journals of examples or insights that occur as they listen.

- What do you think of Wesley's criteria of justice, mercy, and truth?
- Would you add other criteria for evaluating your words?
- Think about what you have read or have posted recently on social media. How does it measure up to the criteria of justice, mercy/compassion, and truth?
- Reflect on the way you talk with the members of your family, your friends, the members of your church, and the various people that you come into contact with. Do these conversations express love, or have they been negative and destructive?

Invite participants to share their responses to the questions.

The Golden Rule

The author shares a quotation from Wesley on the requirement of love (page 43). Read this quotation to the group and invite sharing in pairs about ways they believe this Wesleyan ideal is realistic or impractical. Ask the pairs to share together examples of times that their best intentions and motivations have not had good results. How did that feel? What did they do? Invite the pairs to share insights with the group.

Love and Money

Both the Bible and John Wesley place considerable focus on the ways we use money as an expression of our relationship with God. Post or hand out the following table and invite participants to respond to each statement pair:

Money and the Meaning of Life

(circle the statement in each row
with which you most strongly agree)

Money is a means to an end.	Money is an end in itself.
It is wiser to save for the future.	It is wiser to spend now while you have it.
God will provide.	God helps those who help themselves.
God's blessings are material.	God's blessings are spiritual.
God is the owner, we are the caretakers.	We are the owner of what God gives us.
Giving is a matter of personal choice.	Giving is a mandate to God's people.
Money management is a spiritual issue.	Money management is a secular issue.
Wealthy people are entitled to their wealth.	Wealthy people have a responsibility to share their wealth.
Wealth poses no problem for faithful discipleship.	Wealth is a hindrance to faithful discipleship.
Poverty is a virtue.	Poverty is a curse.
God favors the wealthy.	God favors the poor.

NOTE: *For participants who want to explore the relationship between money and faith more deeply, recommend use of a Money Autobiography. A good one is available at https://doroteos2.com/2015/02/11/money-autobiography/.*

Original Sin, Justification, Sanctification, and Perfection

In the section "The Way of God's Love" (pages 44-49), our author introduces a number of terms significant to Wesleyan spirituality: *original sin, justification, sanctification,* and *perfection.* Form four small teams, and assign each team one of these terms. Ask each team to read the entire section together and then write a definition of the assigned term. Invite them to discuss what is new or surprising in the Wesleyan understanding of the term. Distribute large sheets of paper and markers, and ask each team to select a scribe and a spokesperson.

When the teams have had time to work, invite them to post and share their definitions. After all the definitions have been shared, ask the participants how these terms are related to one another.

God's Transforming Power

Invite participants to reflect and record personal responses to the following questions:

- How has God been at work in me?
- How have I responded to God?
- How have I experienced God's transforming power?
- In what ways do I have the "mind of Christ" and walk as Jesus did?

Invite individuals who are willing to share their stories to do so.

The Means of Grace

The author also introduces us to the following Wesleyan concepts: *the means of grace, works of piety,* and *works of mercy.* Ask participants to share their understanding of these terms. If necessary, review the section "The Means of Growing in Love" on page 49, particularly the five features of the means of grace.

Wrapping Up

Closing Activities

Personal Reflection

Invite participants to reflect in silence on the following questions:
- Is participating in the means of grace—works of piety and works of mercy—a regular part of my life?
- What significant experiences have I had when engaging in the means of grace?
- How can I arrange my life so that the means of grace become a more significant part of it?

After a time for personal reflection, ask if anyone wants to share an insight or story. This is, of course, voluntary.

Preparation for Session Three

Invite participants to reflect on their understanding of *church*. What comes to mind when they hear the word? What are the most significant experiences—positive and negative—they have had with church?

Closing Prayer

Transforming God, help us to open our hearts to your love so that we might understand fully and share joyfully the lessons learned here about the way your love works in and through us to transform the world. Help us to live our lives as reflections of your mercy, truth, and justice. As your church in and for the world, we pray in the name of Jesus the Christ. Amen.

Three

WHERE IS THE CHURCH IN ALL OF THIS?

Planning the Session

Session Goals

As a result of conversations and activities connected with this session, group members should begin to:

- Reflect on biblical passages related to the "church."
- Understand the meaning of the *visible* church and the *universal* church.
- Assess their current role in and contribution to the church.
- Explore John Wesley's teachings on the church and the means of grace.

Biblical Foundation

> The believers devoted themselves to the apostles'
> teaching, to the community, to their shared meals,
> and to their prayers.... All the believers were united
> and shared everything. They would sell pieces of
> property and possessions and distribute the proceeds
> to everyone who needed them.... They shared food
> with gladness and simplicity. They praised God and
> demonstrated God's goodness to everyone.
>
> (Acts 2:42-47)

Special Preparation

- Ask participants to bring their notebooks or electronic journals. Provide writing paper and pens for those who may need them. Also have a variety of Bibles available for those who do not bring one.
- Invite participants to reflect on and journal about the questions noted at the end of session 2. Ask them to consider one insight they might want to share with the group.
- Have available blank paper or construction paper and markers or crayons.
- Have large sheets of paper or whiteboard available for group activity.
- Obtain a set of variously colored pick-up sticks for the Bible study exercise.

Remember that there are more activities than most groups will have time to complete. As leader, you'll want to go over the session in advance and select or adapt the activities you think will work best for your group in the time allotted. Consider your own responses to questions you will pose to the group.

If group members are not familiar with one another, make nametags available.

Getting Started

Welcome

As participants arrive, welcome them to the study and invite them to make use of one of the available Bibles, if they did not bring one.

Opening Prayer

Gracious and loving God, as we share our reflections and learning in this time and place, help us to remember that you are the source and guide for our life as the church. We pray that this time together leads us to more faithful stewardship of your gifts. Amen.

Opening Activities

When all participants have arrived, invite each person to introduce himself or herself by name and to share responses to the questions posed at the end of session 2.

- What comes to mind when you hear the word *church*?
- What is one significant experience—positive or negative— you have had with church?

Do not take notes during the introductions. When the circle is complete, invite volunteers to read the section "Who Are the

People Brought Together?" (page 55). Invite participants to share how their responses compare and contrast with the author's descriptions.

Learning Together

Bible Study and Discussion

Unity in One Body

Invite a volunteer to read Eph 4:1-6 aloud. Share with the group the saying: "In essentials, unity; in non-essentials, liberty; and in all things, charity" (see *Book of Discipline*, ¶103, p. 57). The saying predates Wesley, but it is a helpful shorthand reference to the Wesleyan approach.

Divide into small teams, distribute large sheets of paper and markers, and ask each team to choose a recorder and a spokesperson and to make a list of *essentials* and *non-essentials* within the body of Christ. What must we all believe, do, agree on? What is important, but not essential?

When the teams have had time to work, invite the spokespersons to share their lists. Be sure to ask probing questions after each team shares (what makes this factor or belief or behavior essential?), but avoid judging the correctness or significance of any choice.

Matthew 13 and Pick-up Sticks

Invite a volunteer to read Matt 13:24-30 aloud. Invite another volunteer to read aloud the paragraph in the book related to this parable (beginning with "Wesley's understanding can be seen in his interpretation . . ." in the section "The Visible Face of the Church," pages 57–54). Ask for two volunteers to play "pick-up sticks." Remind them of the object of the game: to pick up all the sticks from the pile, one at a time, without moving other sticks in the pile.

Add this new rule: they may pick up sticks of only one or two colors (depending on the variety of colors available). While the players take turns, invite the rest of the group to choose a side or a color to root for.

When the game is either won or at an impasse, invite the players to share how it felt to separate individual sticks and what added challenge the "new rule" presented. Invite the cheering sections to share how they felt about the colors that "got in the way" of success in the game.

The idea here is to demonstrate the vast diversity within the church; the challenges presented by the task of deciding who is faithful and who is not; the feelings aroused by even well-intentioned discrimination; the overall challenge of seeking unity. Help the group draw parallels to their experiences in congregational life.

Book Study and Discussion

Visible and Invisible

Ask participants to name some of the characteristics of the "public face" of the churches in your community and in the media. What do friends, coworkers, or neighbors think about the church? What are some of the most significant stories you have encountered about "the church" (in social media, conversation, news sources)? Note prominent characteristics on a large sheet of paper under the heading, "The Visible Face of the Church."

Now, invite a volunteer to summarize the main ideas of the section "The Visible Face of the Church," pages 57–64, then give the rest of the group an opportunity to fill in any details or key points the volunteer may have missed. Call the group's attention to the bulleted list on page 61. Ask the group to compare the posted list of the "visible face" of the church with the bulleted list of invisible or universal characteristics in the book. What are the commonalities and differences? What does the visible face of the church say about its invisible life?

Cultivating Love

How do we make the invisible visible? The author shares John Wesley's ideal for the institutional church and then lifts up Wesley's expanded list of "means of grace" as the avenues by which to reach this ideal. Ask participants to review the section "Cultivating Love—The Church and the Means of Grace" on pages 64–68 (if time permits, invite volunteers to read it aloud).

Ask the group, in pairs, to share the means of grace that are most significant in their lives and how their lives have been changed by these practices in community. If people are new to the idea of practicing the means of grace, they can share which practices they would like to try and why.

When the pairs have had time to work, invite participants to share insights.

Wrapping Up

Closing Activities

Personal Reflection

Invite participants to spend a few moments in silent reflection on their experience of the "invisible" or universal church and how it compares with the "visible" or public face of the church. Pose this question: What is one step I can take today to deepen my relationship with God and help make the invisible church visible? Encourage participants to record their step in their journals and practice it before the next session.

Preparation

Point out the terms *covenant, welcoming,* and *missional* at the beginning of chapter 4 in the book. Ask participants to write these terms in their journals, and invite them to record their first impressions or understandings of the terms and to add to and revise their notes as they read chapter 4. Encourage them to include both positive and negative examples from their own church life.

Closing Prayer

Loving God, you call us to the unity of peace as the one body of Christ. Help us to deepen our connection with the universal church and to find new ways to manifest your divine love in the world, so that those who follow us will know your love through us. We are your church, your witness in and for the world, and so we pray in the name of Jesus the Christ. Amen.

Four

WHAT DOES SUCH A CHURCH LOOK LIKE? (1)

Planning the Session

Session Goals

As a result of conversations and activities connected with this session, group members should begin to:

- Reflect on biblical passages related to *covenant, welcome,* and *mission.*
- Understand the meaning of *covenantal community, welcoming community,* and *missional community.*
- Assess their current faith community's witness to God's love in the world.
- Explore John Wesley's teachings on *covenant, welcome,* and *mission.*

Biblical Foundation

> I will make of you a great nation and will bless you. I will make your name respected, and you will be a blessing.
>
> (Gen 12:2)

Special Preparation

- Ask participants to bring their notebooks or electronic journals. Provide writing paper and pens for those who may need them. Also have a variety of Bibles available for those who do not bring one.
- Invite participants to reflect on and journal about the terms listed at the end of session 3.
- Have available blank paper or construction paper and markers or crayons.
- Have large sheets of paper or whiteboard available for group activity.

Remember that there are more activities than most groups will have time to complete. As leader, you'll want to go over the session in advance and select or adapt the activities you think will work best for your group in the time allotted. Consider your own responses to questions you will pose to the group.

If group members are not familiar with one another, make nametags available.

Getting Started

Welcome

As participants arrive, welcome them to the study and invite them to make use of one of the available Bibles, if they did not bring one.

Opening Prayer

Great Lord of blessing, you fill us with your light and make covenant to be our God. Help us to offer the welcome of your love to all people through our lives and ministry, that we might become the blessing of your promise. In Christ's name we pray. Amen.

Opening Activity

When all participants have arrived, invite each person to introduce himself or herself by name and to identify the step he or she chose to make at the end of the last session and how the person has practiced that step. Do not take notes during the introductions.

Learning Together

Bible Study and Discussion

In chapter 4, our author explores three significant expressions of a faithful community of God: *covenant, welcome,* and *mission.* While these often overlap, they also each have distinct characteristics and biblical foundations. Depending on the size of your group and the time available, you may want to do the Bible study exercises one at a time. They are presented here as three similar small-group exercises that can be done simultaneously and then shared.

Split into three small teams and assign each team the biblical texts that help shape their assigned concept. Distribute large sheets of paper and markers. Invite each team to read the related biblical texts and then form together a definition of the concept. They may also draw upon the author's insights from the book and their journal reflections, made since the last session, on the assigned concept *(see "Preparation" at the end of session 3)*. Invite the teams to assign a recorder and a spokesperson.

- Covenant—Gen 17:1-9; 2 Kgs 23:2-3; Jer 31:31-34
- Welcome—Deut 24:17; Mark 9:36-37; Luke 14:7-14; Rom 15:7; Heb 13:1-2
- Mission—Gen 12:2; Matt 25:31-46; Matt 28:18-20; Acts 1:8

When the teams have had time to work, invite the spokespersons to post and share the teams' definitions. When all three teams have shared, ask participants to identity common and unique elements among the definitions.

Book Study and Discussion

The Church as a Covenant Community

The author shares some key Wesleyan features of covenant in the section "The Covenant in Wesley's Theology" (page 75). Invite volunteers to read this bullet list of features and the four assertions that follow. Then pose the question to the group:

- Why was covenant a significant concept in the Wesleyan movement?
- How does the church today (local and denominational) express that it is in covenant relationship with the crucified Lord?

Be sure to examine your own life and church involvement, as well as that of others (it's easy to criticize from a distance).

The Church as a Welcoming Community

Few congregations would describe themselves as "unfriendly," but the author points to Wesley's much more radical understanding of *welcome* as openness to all who seek God, wherever they may be: in the Methodist societies, but also in "the fields, marketplaces, prisons, and wherever else people gathered to hear the message of God's love for all" (see "Early Methodism as an Open Movement," pages 79–82). The author then shares Wesley's commentary on Acts 11:17 and lifts up ways that Methodism has failed in its welcome throughout its history.

Invite the group, in pairs, to review this section in the book and discuss ways that they have experienced or offered radical welcome—Open Hearts, Open Minds, Open Doors—through their congregations. Would some people feel unwelcome if they walked through your doors? Why?

After the pairs have had time to work, invite participants to share insights from their discussion. Invite the group to reflect together on ways they might have contributed to an atmosphere of exclusion. Identify at least one step the congregation and individuals within the congregation can take to increase its welcoming spirit.

The Church as a Missional Community

In the section "Wesley's Understanding of Mission," the author explores four examples of Wesley's understanding of the mission for the church. This is followed by the section "With Wesley and Beyond Wesley: Mission Today" (pages 90–91). Divide into four teams and assign each team one example. Distribute large sheets of paper and markers, and ask them to select a recorder and a spokesperson. Ask each team to review the material related to the assigned example and also the later section, and to reflect on its application in today's church and culture. Include these questions:

- What would it take to make mission central to our local congregations?
- What can be done to foster a vision for mission?
- Apply these questions to the United Methodist connection: the annual conference and the denomination.

The teams can answer the questions in any way they choose except "a list": they can use story, poetry, music, images, mind-maps, even dance.

When the teams have had time to work, invite each spokesperson to post and share the fruit of their team's work.

Wrapping Up

Closing Activity

Covenant Renewal Service

The closing prayer for this session invites the entire group to read together the adaptation of Wesley's covenant prayer, found in *The United Methodist Hymnal*. If time permits, consider observing the entire "Covenant Renewal Service" found in *The United Methodist Book of Worship*, 288. (See the suggestion in session 9 for closing the study with this activity instead.)

Preparation

Post the following terms and invite participants to record them in their journals: *sacrament, countercultural, mutual accountability*. Invite them to record their first impressions or understandings of these terms and to add to and revise their notes as they read chapter 5.

Closing Prayer

Pray together "A Covenant Prayer in the Wesleyan Tradition" from *The United Methodist Hymnal*, 607.

Five

WHAT DOES SUCH A CHURCH LOOK LIKE? (2)

Planning the Session

Session Goals

As a result of conversations and activities connected with this session, group members should begin to:

- Reflect on biblical passages related to Communion, countercultural community, and mutual accountability.
- Understand the meaning of *sacrament*, *countercultural*, and *accountability*.
- Assess their commitment to the call of discipleship.
- Explore John Wesley's teachings on the community as sacramental, countercultural, and accountable through small groups.

Biblical Foundation

"If I, your Lord and teacher, have washed your feet, you too must to wash each other's feet. I have given you an example: Just as I have done, you also must do. . . .

"Love each other. Just as I have loved you, so you also must love each other. This is how everyone will know that you are my disciples, when you love each other."
(John 13:14-15, 34-35)

Special Preparation

• Ask participants to bring their notebooks or electronic journals. Provide writing paper and pens for those who may need them. Also have a variety of Bibles available for those who do not bring one.

• Invite participants to reflect on and journal about the terms and concepts listed at the end of session 4. Ask them to consider one insight they might want to share with the group.

• Have available blank paper or construction paper and markers or crayons.

• Have large sheets of paper or whiteboard available for group activity.

• Have available a current edition of *The Book of Discipline of The United Methodist Church*.

Remember that there are more activities than most groups will have time to complete. As leader, you'll want to go over the session in advance and select or adapt the activities you think will work best for your group in the time allotted. Consider your own responses to questions you will pose to the group.

If group members are not familiar with one another, make nametags available.

Getting Started

Welcome

As participants arrive, welcome them to the study and invite them to make use of one of the available Bibles, if they did not bring one.

Opening Prayer

Loving God, we are yours. We pray that this time of sharing and learning moves us to more cruciform love and more joy-filled living as your countercultural witnesses to the world. In the name of Jesus the Christ, we pray. Amen.

Opening Activity

When all participants have arrived, invite each person to introduce himself or herself by name and to share his or her most memorable experience of Holy Communion. Do not take notes during the introductions.

Learning Together

Bible Study and Discussion

Communion

Share with the group this definition of *sacrament*: "ritual practices that connect us to the mystery of God's love and grace and call us to respond in faith." The United Methodist Church observes the two sacraments specifically commanded by Jesus: baptism and Holy Communion.

Read together Luke 22:14-20. Ask participants if the regular celebration of Holy Communion is a significant aspect of their spiritual life. What about in the life of their congregations? How would they describe the meaning of celebrating Holy Communion?

If time permits and an elder is present, celebrate together the sacrament of Holy Communion, using one of the services of "Word and Table" from *The United Methodist Hymnal* (pages 6–31).*

Countercultural Community

Divide into two teams. Assign each group one of the Bible passages listed below. Ask them to select a spokesperson for the team. Invite the teams to read the passage together and discuss the ways in which it expresses the call to Christians to be countercultural.

- Mark 2:15-28 (Jesus feasts with sinners; John fasts; Sabbath made for humans, not humans for the Sabbath)
- Matt 5:21-48 (the series of Jesus' teachings in the pattern of "You have heard that it was said. . . . But I say to you. . . .")

Mutual Accountability

Invite a volunteer to read aloud John 13:14-15, 34-35. Ask the group to share, in pairs, how Jesus' washing of the disciples' feet and the commandment to love each other call us to mutual accountability in servant leadership.

---

* NOTE: For more information, direct participants to the United Methodist extended statements about the sacraments: *This Holy Mystery* and *By Water and the Spirit*, both available for free download at https://www.umcdiscipleship .org/resources and for purchase through online book retailers. Also of use are United Methodist brochures, including one each on "Holy Communion" and "Baptism."

When the pairs have had time to talk, invite volunteers to share their insights or questions with the larger group.

Book Study and Discussion

Holy Communion and Wesley

In the section "Holy Communion in John Wesley's Theology," the author shares five ways that the regular celebration of Holy Communion was central to John Wesley's theology: communion with Christ, re-presentation of the Crucifixion, conversion, corporate, and future focus (pages 94–96). Read to the group the first paragraph of the section. Then divide into five small teams and assign each team one of the remaining paragraphs. Invite them to read the paragraph together and discuss how this aspect of Wesley's theology relates to (or does not relate to) their experience of the sacrament.

When the teams have had time to work, invite them to share insights from their conversations and any new understandings of the significance of Holy Communion.

Open Communion, Open Community

Summarize for the group, or invite a volunteer to summarize, the story the author tells about Nelson Mandela inviting one of his prison guards to share in the celebration of Holy Communion (page 97). Ask participants to reflect privately for a moment or two on the following questions:

- How does the story make you feel? Do you think you would be capable of offering to share Communion with someone who was your "enemy"?
- What is the significance for you of the United Methodist practice of an "open" table?

- In what ways do you feel in communion with Christ and with others when we celebrate Holy Communion together?

After a short time of personal reflection, invite participants to share their insights and stories.

Countercultural Community

Ask the group members if they agree or disagree with the author's statement, "If United Methodism is to be true to its roots, it will increasingly return to its countercultural heritage" (in the section "A Countercultural Community"; also review the sections "Countercultural Methodism" and "Being Countercultural Today," pages 103–106). How might counterculturalism be expressed through local congregations? through the global denomination? Record group responses on large sheets of paper or whiteboard.

General Rules

In the section "Countercultural Methodism," the author introduces John Wesley's General Rules. Locate these in the *Book of Discipline 2016* (¶104, pages 78–80). Read the rules or provide them as a handout and invite volunteers to read the rules to the group, beginning with "There is only one condition previously required…" (page 78).

Divide into three teams and assign each team one category of the rules: (1) Do no harm; (2) Do good; (3) Attend upon the ordinances of God. Distribute large sheets of paper and markers and ask each team to select a recorder and a spokesperson. Invite the teams to list rules for our time for the assigned category.

When the teams have had time to work, invite the spokespersons to post and share their lists. Invite participant responses, and make additions to the lists as necessary.

Cruciform Love

In the section "Community of the Crucified," the author focuses on the importance of the cross of Christ as a defining aspect of our countercultural identity as Christians (pages 101–103). Invite the group to review, in pairs, the five points the author uses to support this claim, and then to share their responses to the statements. Do they agree or disagree with the author about the centrality of the Crucifixion in Christian life? What is challenging or exciting about the author's claims about the cross?

When the pairs have had time to work, invite them to share insights and questions with the larger group.

Mutual Accountability through Small Groups

Invite a volunteer to read aloud the section "Theology of Small Groups" (pages 107–108). Remind the group that the author then describes the various types of small groups developed by John Wesley—classes, bands, and select societies—for mutual accountability. Form teams of three or four participants, and invite them to share with one another their experiences of small groups in the church, if any. Ask them to reflect on these questions:

- In what ways did my small group experiences relate to my spiritual life?
- What type of small group would I like to experience? What would be beneficial to my relationship with God and others?
- What can I do to help foster a spiritually focused small group in my congregation? Who do I need to contact?

Wrapping Up

Closing Activities

Reflection

Invite participants to ask each other, in pairs, the question, "How is it with your soul?"

Preparation

Post these words and invite participants to note them in their journals: *community on the margins, connectional community,* and *transnational community.* Invite them to record their first impressions or understandings of these terms and to add to and revise their notes as they read chapter 6.

Closing Prayer

Crucified and risen Christ, we have explored, shared, learned, and questioned together. Thank you. Help us to take the lessons from this time into our lives so that people can see your love alive in us. Keep us open to your presence and power and to one another as we seek to manifest your love in self-sacrifice, in countercultural service, and in loving one another; in your name we pray. Amen.

Six

WHAT DOES SUCH A CHURCH LOOK LIKE? (3)

Planning the Session

Session Goals

As a result of conversations and activities connected with this session, group members should begin to:

- Reflect on biblical passages related to faith communities that are *on the margins*, *connectional*, and *transnational*.
- Understand the meaning of *ministry on the margins*, *connectional community*, and *transnational faith community*.
- Assess the effectiveness of their faith communities in these areas.

- Explore John Wesley's teachings on ministry to all and the power of connection.

Biblical Foundation

> There is neither Greek nor Jew, circumcised nor uncircumcised, barbarian, Scythian, slave nor free, but Christ is all things and in all people.
>
> (Col 3:11)

Special Preparation

- Ask participants to bring their notebooks or electronic journals. Provide writing paper and pens for those who may need them. Also have a variety of Bibles available for those who do not bring one.
- Invite participants to reflect on and journal about the terms and concepts listed at the end of session 5. Ask them to consider one insight they might want to share with the group.
- Have available blank paper or construction paper and markers or crayons.
- Have large sheets of paper or whiteboard available for group activity.

Remember that there are more activities than most groups will have time to complete. As leader, you'll want to go over the session in advance and select or adapt the activities you think will work best for your group in the time allotted. Consider your own responses to questions you will pose to the group.

If group members are not familiar with one another, make nametags available.

Getting Started

Welcome

As participants arrive, welcome them to the study and invite them to make use of one of the available Bibles, if they did not bring one.

Opening Prayer

Lord of all creation, we join together to seek your will for our lives and for our congregations. Help us to see past all barriers to the light of your glory in all and through all. In Christ's name we pray. Amen.

Opening Activity

When all participants have arrived, invite each person to introduce himself or herself by name and to share a time he or she has felt excluded, isolated, or marginalized. Do not take notes during the introductions.

Learning Together

Bible Study and Discussion

Community on the Margins

In the section "Insights from Wesley" (pages 114–117), the author points to the language of 1 Cor 4:13 as the source for Wesley's language in the first General Rule. This verse is actually part of Paul's admonishment of the Corinthian church for being spoiled and soft.

Invite a volunteer to read aloud 1 Cor 4:1-13. As the text is read, invite participants to consider a time they have felt excluded or marginalized (as they shared in the opening activity).

Invite the group, in pairs, to share their responses to the following questions:

- Do you relate more closely with the Corinthian Christians or with Paul? Why?
- In what way does this biblical call—to take up your cross in the face of persecution—affect your feelings about the experience of being excluded or marginalized?

Connectional Community

One of the prominent features of The United Methodist Church is our connectional system. Connectionalism has biblical roots. Invite volunteers to read Acts 15:1-29, the account of the Jerusalem Council.

As the passage is read, invite participants to note elements of connectionalism that reflect our modern United Methodist system. What works well, and where is there room for improvement?

Colossians and Transnational Community

Invite participants to review the section "A Biblical Reflection: The Letter to the Colossians" (pages 127–129). Divide into teams of three or four, and ask each team to discuss the following questions:

- Who are the equivalents of the barbarians and the Scythians in your social, political, and cultural context?
- Can you imagine them as part of your congregation?
- What would it take for your congregation to include them?

When the teams have had time to work, invite them to share the collective wisdom of their group discussion.

Book Study and Discussion

Enlarging the Circle

Invite participants to name groups or individuals in their local community, work, social circle, or church who experience deprivation, exploitation, exclusion, and rejection. When you have generated a list on paper or whiteboard, invite the group to reflect, in pairs, on how the church does, or can, engage, minister with, stand with, and serve these people and groups.

When the pairs have had time to work, invite them to share insights and ideas. Note these on paper or whiteboard, and invite the participants to select at least one step to act on in their contexts.

Connectionalism

The author gives a history of connectionalism as a significant aspect of Methodism. Under the section "Key Features of Connectionalism," he further explores components of connectionalism (pages 122–126). Divide into three teams, and assign one of the following terms to each team: *itineracy, conference, superintendency*. Distribute large sheets of paper and markers, and ask each team to select a recorder and a spokesperson.

Invite each team to read the material in the book related to the assigned term and reflect on the following:

- How is this feature of connectionalism expressed in The United Methodist Church?
- What does this feature say about the identity and mission of The United Methodist Church?
- If you could do so, what would you change and why?

When the teams have had time to work, invite the spokespersons to share the insights and understandings of the group.

Are We a Transnational Community?

The author shares a variety of ways that the ministry of The United Methodist Church is expressed and experienced around the globe. Invite participants to share stories of their experiences with congregations or ministries from other parts of the world. Perhaps group members have had extensive interaction with global United Methodism, and the shared stories will be a deep source of enrichment on their own.

If not, or if some group members have limited experience with international ministry, post the following questions for reflection and discussion:

- What does it mean to you and your congregation that you are part of a transnational church? Does it have any significance? What have you gained from it? What opportunities does it provide for you and your church?
- How does loyalty to Christ the crucified Lord question and critique our loyalty to our own nation and its leaders?
- If in Christ there is "neither Greek nor Jew . . . barbarian [nor] Scythian," then our relationship with our fellow *Christians* is closer than that with our fellow *citizens*. What does this mean for the way we relate to our own country?
- What does it mean to be in connection with fellow Christians who are negatively affected by the forces of globalization that benefit us?
- How do we express solidarity with our fellow United Methodists in other countries?
- What is the particular challenge to United Methodists as members of a transnational church?

Wrapping Up

Closing Activities

Reflection

Invite a volunteer to read aloud the chapter conclusion (page 133). Ask participants to reflect, in silence, on how this description of The United Methodist Church is expressed in and through their congregations and what it means for their personal lives of faith. Ask them to note responses in their journals.

Preparation

Invite a volunteer to read the introductory paragraph of chapter 7. Ask group members to consider the following questions as they read the chapter in preparation for the next session:

- How do you understand the unity of the church?
- Do you think it is important that this unity be visible to the world?

Closing Prayer

God of all people and all nations, we are humbled by the enormity of your call to sacrificial ministry. Give us the courage to stand with those without voice, to reach out to those in need, to seek deeper connection with our global brothers and sisters. We strive, Lord, we strive; and we pray in Christ's name. Amen.

Seven

THE VISIBLE UNITY
OF THE CHURCH

Planning the Session

Session Goals

As a result of conversations and activities connected with this session, group members should begin to:

- Reflect on biblical passages related to *unity.*
- Understand the meaning of *unity* and *diversity.*
- Assess their level of devotion to the unity of the church.
- Explore John Wesley's teachings on *unity, diversity,* and *transformation.*

Biblical Foundation

> "I pray they will be one, Father, just as you are in me and I am in you. I pray that they also will be in us, so that the world will believe that you sent me." (John 17:21)

Special Preparation

- Ask participants to bring their notebooks or electronic journals. Provide writing paper and pens for those who may need them. Also have a variety of Bibles available for those who do not bring one.
- Invite participants to reflect on and journal about the terms and concepts listed at the end of session 6. Ask them to consider one insight they might want to share with the group.
- Have available blank paper or construction paper and markers or crayons.
- Have large sheets of paper or whiteboard available for group activity.

Remember that there are more activities than most groups will have time to complete. As leader, you'll want to go over the session in advance and select or adapt the activities you think will work best for your group in the time allotted. Consider your own responses to questions you will pose to the group.

If group members are not familiar with one another, make nametags available.

Getting Started

Welcome

As participants arrive, welcome them to the study and invite them to make use of one of the available Bibles, if they did not bring one.

Opening Prayer

Lord of each and all, unite us in ministry. Help us to learn the universal language of love even as we embrace our diversity. In Christ's name we pray. Amen.

Opening Activity

When all participants have arrived, invite each person to introduce himself or herself by name and to share a definition of *unity in the church*. Do not take notes during the introductions.

Learning Together

Bible Study and Discussion

Unity at Ephesus and Today

Ask group members to review the section "A Biblical Reflection" (pages 137–139), and invite a volunteer to read aloud Eph 2:11-22.

Ask participants to respond to the question: In today's world, what does it mean to claim that there are "no longer strangers and aliens" in our communities of faith?

Book Study and Discussion

Wesley on Unity

The author shares some Wesleyan perspectives on the critical importance of unity in the church. Divide into teams of three or four, and ask each team to review the section "A Wesleyan Perspective" (pages 139–142). Invite them to discuss the following:

- Do you agree or disagree with the author's statement of Wesley's view that "the visible unity of the church exemplifies what it means to be the church"?

- What is more important, *unity* or *holiness* (right belief or right action)? Why?

When the groups have had time to work, invite them to share the responses and insights shared in the group discussion.

A Missional Imperative

In the section "Visible Unity Is a Missional Imperative," the author declares, "It is not that the church *has* a mission, the church *is* the mission. . . . Its unity in contrast to worldly divisions and strife is a sign of the reality of God's love and an integral component of its mission in the world" (pages 142–144). Invite the group to review the section, and then discuss:

- What form should church unity take?
- Does unity require the federation of all denominations?
- Is this practical or even desirable?
- How is the church doing as a visible witness to unity?

Embracing Diversity

In the section "Diversity: A Means of Grace," the author shares Wesley's views on the "catholic" (universal) nature of loving community (pages 144–147). He then makes the claim that "Participation in a theologically diverse community can become a means of grace when approached as an opportunity to express deep love for those with whom we disagree" (page 146).

Invite the group, in pairs, to reflect on this claim that diversity can be a means of grace. Use the following questions as prompts to conversation:

- Who, in your immediate Christian context, do you strongly disagree with?
- Do you love these people?

- How is that reflected in the way you interact with them?
- How have your differences with people been a blessing to you and helped your faith to grow?

When the pairs have had time to share, invite them to offer insights and new understandings to the larger group.

Wesleyan Essentials

In his section on "Centers and Boundaries," the author discusses five key doctrines of Wesley's theology: *original sin, prevenient grace, justification and assurance, new birth,* and *sanctification* (pages 150–151). Divide into five teams, and assign one of the doctrines to each team. Distribute sheets of paper and markers, and ask the teams to select recorders and spokespersons. Ask each team to read the material related to the assigned doctrine and to explore together the following:

- How would we restate this doctrine in our terms?
- Why is this a core doctrine in Wesleyan theology?
- Do we agree that this doctrine is central to a transformed life of Christian love? Why or why not?

When the teams have had time to work, invite the spokespersons to share the findings of their teams.

Once all the teams have shared, discuss the following questions together.

- What are (or should be) the core beliefs of Christianity? of United Methodism?
- On what moral and ethical issues should all United Methodists (or all Christians) agree? How do they relate to the core beliefs?

Wrapping Up

Closing Activities

Reflection

Invite participants to reflect, in silence, on a relationship or issue in the church that has been a source of tension or conflict. Have they responded or reacted in love or in anger? Is it time to seek reconciliation? What is one step they will take toward deeper unity and harmony? Encourage them to record their planned step in their journals.

Preparation

Invite a volunteer to read the opening paragraphs of chapter 8, and invite participants to reflect on these questions as they prepare for the next session:

- "Is it possible to be part of the same church with people we believe have fundamentally false ideas about who God is, what God is doing, and how Jesus fits into the larger picture?" (page 155).
- What key issues are sources of disagreement in your local congregation?
- How is your congregation handling the disagreements?

If you are not doing a ninth session, invite participants to read both chapter 8 and the book's conclusion in advance of the next session.

Closing Prayer

Lord of one and Lord of all, guide our thoughts and our hearts, so that our actions and our words lead to deeper unity in your love. We ask this humbly in Jesus' name. Amen.

Eight
CAN WE BE ONE COMMUNITY?

Planning the Session

Session Goals

As a result of conversations and activities connected with this session, group members should begin to:

- Reflect on biblical passages related to managing conflicts in the church.
- Understand the meaning of *holiness*; *sin, properly so called*; and *holy conferencing*.
- Assess their relationships with the money they give and share.
- Explore John Wesley's teachings on giving all we can.

Biblical Foundation

If possible, to the best of your ability, live at peace with all people. (Rom 12:18)

Special Preparation

- Ask participants to bring their notebooks or electronic journals. Provide writing paper and pens for those who may need them. Also have a variety of Bibles available for those who do not bring one.
- Invite participants to reflect on and journal about the questions listed at the end of session 7. Ask them to consider one insight they might want to share with the group.
- Have available blank paper or construction paper and markers or crayons.
- Have large sheets of paper or whiteboard available for group activity.

Remember that there are more activities than most groups will have time to complete. As leader, you'll want to go over the session in advance and select or adapt the activities you think will work best for your group in the time allotted. Consider your own responses to questions you will pose to the group.

If group members are not familiar with one another, make nametags available.

Getting Started

Welcome

As participants arrive, welcome them to the study and invite them to make use of one of the available Bibles, if they did not bring one.

Opening Prayer

Great God of peace, you call us to reconciliation through the healing power of your Holy Spirit. Open our hearts to your grace, Lord. Open our minds in this time of learning and sharing. We pray in Jesus' name. Amen.

Opening Activity

When all participants have arrived, invite each person to introduce himself or herself by name and to share an example of a disagreement in the church with which he or she has personal experience. Do not take notes during the introductions.

Learning Together

Bible Study and Discussion

Dealing with Controversy

The author offers "A Biblical Reflection" on Rom 14, in which he notes the importance of the motivations that drive our behavior (pages 169–172). Ask for volunteers to read this section of the text aloud, and then invite responses to the following:

- What are some of the recurring themes of conflict in many congregations today?
- In what way do Paul's arguments in Rom 14 provide avenues of resolution and help people with differing views live together in harmony?
- How can a conflict become an opportunity for spiritual growth?

Book Study and Discussion

Holiness

In the section "The Catholic Spirit or Holiness in a Diverse Church" (pages 159–163), the author states, "Holiness requires an integration of belief and action: deep commitment to what one holds to be true, clear rejection of what one believes to be erroneous, and a way of treating others who see things differently." Invite a volunteer to read this statement aloud.

Divide into three teams and assign each team one aspect of the integration of belief and action that leads to holiness:

- Deep commitment to what one holds to be true
- Clear rejection of what one believes to be erroneous
- A way of treating others who see things differently

Ask each team to create an expression of the assigned aspect in images, story, poetry, or music. The presentation should embody the "integration of belief and action," motivated by the "one heart" of mutual love and respect.

When the teams have had time to work, invite them to share their presentations. Encourage participants to share the challenges of the assignment and how they worked together to meet them.

Sin, Properly So Called

In the section "Theological Roots" (pages 164–169), the author explores Wesleyan understandings of our human frailty and the limitations of being embodied creatures. In the course of the discussion, he distinguishes willing violation of the will of God from involuntary sin.

Ask for volunteers to read aloud the section "Sin, Properly So Called" (pages 166–167). Invite the group, in pairs, to discuss the Wesleyan perspective on sin. Offer the following questions:

- Do you agree that some sin is forgivable even without confession and repentance, and some is not?
- What is our responsibility in understanding the difference?
- Who is responsible to judge those who sin?
- What is our proper response to people with whom we disagree?

When the pairs have had some time to share, invite them to offer insights gained from their discussion.

Holy Conferencing

The author revisits the themes of *truth, mercy,* and *justice* through the lens of the Wesleyan practice of holy conferencing. Invite volunteers to read aloud the first paragraphs of the section "Practical Fruits: Holy Conferencing" (pages 172–176). Ask participants:

- Why did John Wesley consider holy conferencing to be a means of grace?
- How is holy conferencing different from other kinds of conversation?
- What makes holy conferencing an effective approach to debate and controversy?

Review and Next Steps

If you are not doing a ninth session, take some time to review insights and learnings from the study. If you are doing a ninth session, skip this section and go to "Wrapping Up," below.

Invite participants to share one concept or idea from the study that surprised them or was brand-new to them.

Ask participants to share positive steps they have taken or plan to take—in their personal lives and their congregations—to build unity and foster visible expressions of divine love.

Ask for volunteers to read aloud the closing paragraphs of the book's conclusion (pages 181–183). As the paragraphs are read, invite group members to note their responses to the terms *repentance, lament, thanksgiving,* and *new hope.*

Finally, ask group members to share stories of the good things the church is both being and doing in their context.

Close the session by again reading together "A Covenant Prayer in the Wesleyan Tradition," from *The United Methodist Hymnal*, 607.

Wrapping Up

Closing Activities

Reflection

Invite participants to read silently and reflect on the "Summary" bullet list at the end of the section "Theological Roots" (pages 168–169). Ask them to note in their journals plans for improvement in any areas of weakness they encounter in the list.

Preparation

If you are doing a ninth session, invite participants to read the book's conclusion and review their journal notes in advance of the final session.

Closing Prayer

Gracious and loving God, make us one in Christ, one with each other, and one in ministry to all the world. Through the power of your Holy Spirit and in the name of the risen Christ we pray. Amen.

Nine

OUR PURPOSE IS LOVE: CONCLUSION

Planning the Session

Session Goals

As a result of conversations and activities connected with this session, group members should begin to:

- Reflect on biblical passages related to love as our Christian purpose.
- Understand the meaning of *lament, repentance, thanksgiving, and new hope.*
- Assess their growth in faith through the course of the study.
- Review John Wesley's teachings on love as our Christian purpose.

Biblical Foundation

God is love. (1 John 4:8)

Special Preparation

- Ask participants to bring their notebooks or electronic journals. Provide writing paper and pens for those who may need them. Also have a variety of Bibles available for those who do not bring one.
- Invite participants to reflect on and journal about the terms and concepts listed at the end of session 8. Ask them to consider one insight they might want to share with the group.
- Have available blank paper or construction paper and markers or crayons.
- Have large sheets of paper or whiteboard available for group activity.

Remember that there are more activities than most groups will have time to complete. As leader, you'll want to go over the session in advance and select or adapt the activities you think will work best for your group in the time allotted. Consider your own responses to questions you will pose to the group.

If group members are not familiar with one another, make nametags available.

Getting Started

Welcome

As participants arrive, welcome them to the study and invite them to make use of one of the available Bibles, if they did not bring one.

Opening Prayer

Great God of love, open our hearts, our minds, our hands, and our eyes, to see and to be your love in and for the world. In the name of Christ, we pray. Amen.

Opening Activity

When all participants have arrived, invite each person to introduce himself- or herself by name and to share one new insight he or she has gained during the study. Do not take notes during the introductions.

Learning Together

Bible Study and Discussion

A Journey of Love

Post or provide on a handout the biblical foundation verses provided throughout the study. They are printed at the end of this session. Invite participants to select the verses that have deep meaning for them. Ask them to share why these are important verses to them.

Book Study and Discussion

Review and Next Steps

Invite participants to share one concept or idea from the study that surprised them or was brand-new to them. What was surprising or new about this idea? How will it shape their understanding, attitudes, or actions going forward?

Ask group members to share stories of the good things the church is both being and doing in their context.

Continuing the Journey

Ask for volunteers to read aloud the closing paragraphs of the book's conclusion (pages 181–183). As the paragraphs are read, invite group members to note their responses to the terms *repentance, lament, thanksgiving,* and *new hope.* When the paragraphs have been read, invite the group members to share their understanding of these terms.

Ask participants to share positive steps they have taken or plan to take—in their personal lives and their congregations—to build unity, and foster visible expressions of divine love.

Wrapping Up

Closing Activities

Covenant Renewal Service and Communion

If you have not shared together in the Covenant Renewal Service (*Book of Worship,* 288), plan to do so as you close this final session. Incorporate a celebration of Holy Communion, if at all possible.

Closing Prayer

If time does not allow for the full Covenant Renewal Service, close the study by reading together "A Covenant Prayer in the Wesleyan Tradition," from *The United Methodist Hymnal,* 607.

Our Purpose Is Love
Biblical Foundation Verses

Session 1	God created humanity in God's own image, in the divine image God created them, male and female God created them. (Gen 1:27)
Session 2	*"You must love the Lord your God with all your heart, with all your being, with all your strength, and with all your mind, and love your neighbor as yourself."* (Luke 10:27)
Session 3	The believers devoted themselves to the apostles' teaching, to the community, to their shared meals, and to their prayers.... All the believers were united and shared everything. They would sell pieces of property and possessions and distribute the proceeds to everyone who needed them.... They shared food with gladness and simplicity. They praised God and demonstrated God's goodness to everyone. (Acts 2:42-47)
Session 4	I will make of you a great nation and will bless you. I will make your name respected, and you will be a blessing. (Gen 12:2)
Session 5	"If I, your Lord and teacher, have washed your feet, you too must to wash each other's feet. I have given you an example: Just as I have done, you also must do.... "Love each other. Just as I have loved you, so you also must love each other. This is how everyone will know that you are my disciples, when you love each other." (John 13:14-15, 34-35)
Session 6	There is neither Greek nor Jew, circumcised nor uncircumcised, barbarian, Scythian, slave nor free, but Christ is all things and in all people. (Col 3:11)
Session 7	"I pray they will be one, Father, just as you are in me and I am in you. I pray that they also will be in us, so that the world will believe that you sent me." (John 17:21)
Session 8	If possible, to the best of your ability, live at peace with all people. (Rom 12:18)
Session 9	God is love. (1 John 4:8)

CPSIA information can be obtained
at www.ICGtesting.com
Printed in the USA
LVOW10s0518290318
571534LV00012B/135/P

9 781501 868696